Bone Monkey

Janet Sutherland

To Jeremy,
Love & best wishes
Janet x.

Bone Monkey

Shearsman Books

First published in the United Kingdom in 2014 by
Shearsman Books
50 Westons Hill Drive
Emersons Green
BRISTOL
BS16 7DF

Shearsman Books Ltd Registered Office
30–31 St. James Place, Mangotsfield, Bristol BS16 9JB
(this address not for correspondence)

www.shearsman.com

ISBN 978-1-84861-347-8

ACKNOWLEDGEMENTS
Acknowledgements are due to the editors of the following publications in
which some of these poems or earlier versions have appeared:
*Long Poem Magazine, Mslexia, The North, Poetry Review, Poetry Wales,
The Rialto, Shadowtrain, Shearsman, Tears in the Fence.*

I wish to thank Arts Council England for their Award in 2010-2011
which funded a period of inspirational mentoring by Fiona Sampson.
I am indebted to Fiona for her unfailingly generous support and advice.
I am grateful to the Brighton Group who have read many of these poems
as they appeared: Maria Jastrzębska, Robert Hamberger, Lee Harwood,
John McCullough, Bernadette Cremin, Jackie Wills and
Robert Dickinson.
My grateful thanks also to Mimi Khalvati, Clare Best and Catherine
Smith, and to Kay Syrad who lent me a room to work in on Mondays
where some of these poems were written.

'On Your Back' and 'Asssemblage des Beautés' were previously published
in *Hangman's Acre* (Shearsman Books, 2009).

Nearly to the axletrees in sand

I awoke from a sound sleep
the pitching and tossing

had ceased
and now   stuck fast

in opal light
we opened our mouths

amphibious children
of the night

to let the cold come in
our voices strange

even to us
who have been used

to travelling dangerously
Ge thouu, geshvinkt thouu

as we were taught
we entreat them

at last the farm horses
buck and leap with teeth bared

and shivering
gain a firm purchase

"the shadow" represents all that is instinctive in us. Whatever has a tail and lots of hair is in the shadow… Old cave impulses go there, longings to eat the whole world…"

Robert Bly, *A little Book on the Human Shadow*

Contents

A little rhyme before sleep

Roiled by wind and the undertow of tide
the river raises snakes that writhe and glide.
Headlights from the bridge and street lamps
on both banks   silver the ridges on their spines
and gild their flanks.   Where are they going
on this bleak November night?   In whose house
will they gather when the dark runs out?

Up the stairs they slither to the sleeper in his bed—
the slack jawed drowser who has nothing in his head.

All I dream is water
leaf green   brown
I open my mouth
I choke   I drown

Prequel

Out of the void of chaos came the Earth
and then Bone Monkey sprang to life.
Three strands of darkness and a streak of light
were wound inside his head. His heart
made what it could of that. At least it chattered on
in rhythm with the shrieks of other forms
dragged from the reek and mire to consciousness.
Faced with this fait accompli what to do?
He's dissident the moment he takes breath.
The other creatures formulate a knowing god
and stand or lie in awe of her. And start to sing.
The noise is indescribable. He reaches past
this schism, starts to laugh—he's laughing
on a mud ball spinning through the dark.

The Blacksmith made me

With blazing tongs he clamped my head
and cut it off, sliced up my flesh and jointed me.
As big as half the earth, a cauldron hung above his fire.
He threw me in the pot to make his stew.

So three years passed—I simmered and my fat
rose to the surface and was skimmed away.

Next day he ladled out my bones and working fast
he put them in his fire below the coals
and when I blanched and spat he took me
to his anvil and he struck three massive blows.

And then I sang. I was a bell
and when he plunged me in his trough I was the sea.

The blacksmith made me who I am. He took
my naked bones and covered them. My skull was bare,
his iron hand put in obsidian eyes and lanced my ears,
so down through all the years I'd imitate the speech of man.

Red Hibiscus

Once as Bone Monkey walked the forest paths
a travelling man appeared and spoke to him.

Which of these packets will you have? He asked,
raising two parcels for our friend to choose.

The first was large, imposing, wrapped in leaves
and dressed with a red hibiscus bloom.

*This one has knives, a looking glass and beads
paper and ink, cloth, all you could need.*

The other package swung from his little finger
wrapped in rough cloth and smaller than his thumb.

Immortal Life he said, *is held within
and you can take which bundle you would like.*

I'll have the largest, please Bone Monkey said
and straightaway unwrapped the gift,

picked out the prettiest knife, to test the blade,
and plunged it in his benefactor's chest.

I'll take the smallest too, he told his host
and stole it from the dead man's open palm.

Skull bowl decorated with a silver band repoussé monkey heads and Latin script

I was dead and have returned
to life, profane and virtuous
my bones were cleansed,
but still, unhealed, I stalk the earth.

Male écorché leaning against a tree
exposing the anatomy of thorax and left breast
François Jallat 1545

It could be a self portrait, Bone Monkey thinks,
as he considers the picture in its glass case.

He likes the attitude the man has struck
as he holds his peeled skin away from his chest,

his air of worldliness, his open smile,
his calm acceptance of nakedness.

Emblems from the Wolves

Bone Monkey swaggers through a plain of thorns
crowned with insignia of warlike deeds—
emblems stolen from the wolves
are fixed securely to his skull with cords.

His war pipes are a swan's wing bones.
His headdress—raven, magpie, eagle, crow—
chitters behind him. Whispering as he goes,
he says "all I have dreamed is this

and now all I can dream is this".
Bundles of wormwood scour sun and moon
but nothing now is ever as it seemed.
As darkness grows

he lies down in a hollow in the hills
his tattered ribcage—a bowl of stars.

Apollo, Marsyas, Bone Monkey

Intricate work; those long ears,
the pocks on his bulbous nose,
took patience and a steady hand.

The intimate folds and crevices
were tender and whitened with yeast.
He was thorough and took his time.

*

The pelt lay on the mountain slope
where Apollo dropped it, like a red river.
Bone Monkey picked it up and pulled it on.

He drew those tissue lips to his.
When he played,
the flute remembered him.

*

Wild music, hurled with stones
by cataracts in Spring or
hushed with eddies in the shallows of a bay.

In stops, in starts, a blackbird's song.
Drawing the liquid from his throat
on a sunlit post at the edge of any clearing.

As a god

Bone Monkey knows himself a god
although his raddled arms, his ruined balls
and buttocks seem to say he's less than that.
The strings and sinews slacken every day.
His fingers aren't reliable for counting on.
One of them is always loose. His toes
and heels mark out the dust like brogues.
You'd track him from the patterns in his bones,
stalk him to his lair. He's the bogeyman,
the bog man, anaerobically preserved—
but open for inspection. Look at him!
See how the light springs from his beating heart.
Why would a god deny time's ravages?

His exposition on the art of memory

I think of memory
the way I think of men
advancing and retreating

over fields and fens
pikeman and reaper
swept away

I see them falling
as they fall
they turn

*

they fall like puppets
from their strings
pricked by a blade

I envy them
this skill
falling to nothingness

*

I think of memory
as a stain
no matter how I scrub

it doesn't disappear
graffiti on a wall
an aerosol's ejaculate

scrawled
in a stranger's
bloody curlicues

*

I think of memory
as I think of sex
I'd skewer her to still the itch

climb on and poke
her foetid purse
and blaze

a phosphorous
incendiary—
a mortar shell

then in the dark
climb off
still ravenous

*

I think of memory
like a palimpsest
my page pared back

my chronicle
a pumice flour
or drowned in milk

its shadow exiled
under flesh   mysterious—
I think of bones

*

I think of memory
as I think of sleep
a blanket

I'd lie under
in the dark
a roughened skin

sweetened by sweat
and the stink of fear
and by my breath

which cooling clings
as dew does
to a field of grass

*

I think of memory
like three swans that sweep
over the river's surface

ghosts
of the aerial
and of the deep

or like the rivers' flow
tidal and complex
at an estuary

*

I think of memory
as I think of snow
an incremental increase

with each flake
shadow on shadow
in the headlights' glow

*

I think of memory
the way I think of stone
or of ammonites

within that stone
like galaxies
solidified in space

they hold a shape
a shadowing
a hollow where

a beating heart
might one day
cease to beat

*

I think of death
my whitened skull
scraped clean

my heart a pocket-book
my tool
a useless twig

and all that
blows across
my bones

is time
and any memories
are yours

In the beginning

Bone Monkey had grown old—the time had come
to shuck his skin, to slither out plump as a suckling pig,
to slip home leaping like a lord.

The air was full of bright birds fluttering, rose madder
red and cerulean blue, and all the vines grew strong.
The bees were drunk with nectar as they sang.

He took his stick and limped out to the stream
where the low branches made a secret place to hide
and slit the shrivelled leather at his throat.

He put his hands inside, spread them apart
and climbed outside himself. New tender flesh
smelt of ambrosia and was sweetly curved.

He cast his old husk on the waters, watched it sink
and fill and ride, over the shining pebbles
to the shore. It lay before him like a lens,

the gloved hands clapping to the music
of the waves, as minnows whipped between them
in a shoal. He fished it out and dressed himself again.

An Evangelist

en route
to a convention
promises
Bone Monkey
eternal life

Bone Monkey on the art of colour

a rose at the edge
of a parched lawn
pruned for these open cups

catches the throat—
this still afternoon
smells peppery

though *I can't*
smell anything
he says

and a breath of air
in the lungs—
an old man's

feather of breath
sets white rags
falling

How the Monkey found his voice

Bone Monkey discovered his voice
in the Forkhead box protein P2.
He said *Let me tell you, I'd rather be dead
than spend any more time with you.*

Bone Monkey in Love

1

She takes Bone Monkey as a lover

his yellow nails rake down her side
in welted lines that raise and grey
he loves me/loves me not she wails

he takes her out to eat and tells
the other diners she's so fat
says she's the one who worships him

he's brushed her hair until it flies
to flirt with his remaining strands
she hides the bruises   most of them

in bed he slides his narrow leg
between her thighs   he mounts her
as she sleeps and in her sleep she cries

he rocks her   rocks her   riding
all her dreams   he loves her
loves her not

2

Chuman

The scan makes her
translucent
He can see the wall
of her womb

and the fine boned
thing that plays there

She's thick with child—
It might be his
Can he shake her
like a rattle?

3

Lullaby

Who'd want a daddy like me? he croons
to the small bones cradled against his chest,
the thin bones smeared with her blood and muck,
the slight bones rooting for a nipple to suck.

Who'd want a daddy like me? he croons
to the small pulse ticking at its crown
to the brain below that's not his own,
and the softness where there is no bone.

Who'd want a daddy like me? he croons
and rinses the stink of the mother away,
offers his teat to its searching mouth,
and feels it tug and worry for the truth.

Who'd want a daddy like me? he croons
to the eyes that open to stare him out.

4

Our lady of the feathers

Our lady of the feathers
is walking down the street
carrying white wings
the colour of wood anemones.

Our lady of the feathers
is eating a white peach
and her hair's tied back
in a ponytail. Swish, swish

says the pony tail. Our lady
of the feathers has a moleskin
mole on her shoulder
and moleskin hair on her cheek.

Her hips are rounded, her jeans
are tight and white feathers
nuzzle at her breast;
sleepy wood anemones.

Swish, swish say the white
wood anemones in her arms.
Swish, swish say her moleskin
sneakers to the white peach.

5

Seven for the Seven Stars in the Sky

Seven dolls with seven smiles
standing in a row
the biggest bought a Waltzer ride
a spinning boy whipped her hide
so she fell down

Six dolls with six smiles
standing in a row
the biggest met a chat room mate
he's sweet fourteen and fifty-eight
so she fell down

Five dolls with five smiles
standing in a row
the biggest hitched from A to B
with Messrs. C and D and E
so she fell down

Four dolls with four smiles
standing in a row
the biggest stole away to sea
for kisses damp and feathery
so she fell down

Three dolls with three smiles
standing in a row
the biggest did what Simon said

and Simon said lie down, you're dead
so she fell down

Two dolls with two smiles
standing in a row
the biggest never left a note
she just went out, without a coat
so she fell down

One doll with one smile
standing all alone
was Daddy's biggest, bestest girl
his South Sea pearl
so she fell down

6

Desire Lines

The dark breaks open a long scar
from heart to groin. The skin is peeled

to the tenderest flesh, peeled and peeled

though your finger drawing down the line
finds that path of least resistance.

Amulet

A purse dyed red with dried and powdered scarlet grain
worn leather neck cord folded amulet within
(5cm x 6cm)

*

the skin unfolds in three dead languages
not yet interpreted but pictographs

present him seated   standing   capering
within a solid rectangle as if the line

could curb him   fragile as it is
and broken now with age where folding

cracked the ink   look how his hand
grasps at the very edges   of this amulet

The 'infinite monkey' theory is flawed

How many monkeys working every hour
could type the works of Shakespeare
word for word without a typo, faultless,
line by line? Bone Monkey takes the bait

and goes to town. He buys a laptop in the sales
and writes a sonnet in an afternoon.
One glorious *little song* that blows his mind!
As one who walks with death he knows the score,

the dead are silent and their hands are still
darkness approaches and is measureless—
why should he copy-type a stranger's masterpiece?
Why be a thoughtless conduit not a well?

Subversive lines unfold, his fingers fly
and seize the flaming substance of the world.

Left in the dark

One day Bone Monkey read in the local rag about an old man who'd wandered naked at three in the morning from his house in the suburbs, driven his scooter the wrong way down the bypass and been brought back by the police to his wife at ten in the morning: My old dad, he said, trying out the phrase as he ate his toast, drank his morning tea and settled down to the crossword, though having leapt into the world unencumbered he thought more about his own heart and the state of his body hair than about any other old gent come to hard times. Mental gymnastics kept his own mind supple, and his body seemed to take care of itself; his ticker showed no sign of giving out and even on exploratory jaunts up Ben Nevis, that mountain with its head in the clouds, where he tested the limits of his endurance by walking the Carn Mor Dearg Arete in his plimsolls, he'd only been bothered by the cold mist seeping in through the cracks in his privates.

Quick as a flash he solved *Made a dug-out, buried, and passed away* (4) and thought he half fitted the description. *Left in the dark* (8) summed him up perfectly—synapses firing he filled all the blanks with a pencil…

That old boy, on his warm summer's ride down the dual carriageway, was like a latter day cowboy spurring his jittery horse and stepping out into desert. Bone Monkey imagined him gripping his handlebars as he stared fiercely at the road ahead, his eyes tearing in the wind, his electric motor whining its thin songs to the moon.

Bone Monkey at the Allotment

"I can give a dead man almost any look"
                    —John Hunter (1728 –1793)

A light breeze is blowing down at the allotments
Bone Monkey listens to the pea pods rattle
They have a hollow sound   little drums
But are green   so juicy

They sound dry but they're not—
light seeps through
each lime green scrim;
The litter's harnessed to an edge

their short umbilicals
allow a little play
they dance as shadows
fattening slowly in their pen

until they make it dark.
His nail has dipped and bitten into flesh
that so often happens he mutters
as he rubs the peapods one against the other

Lying under white-currant bushes
he's mangy as the fox that stooped and jumped
and came like a ghost to the back door
stopping in daylight
where the babies were beginning
to haul themselves up
at the point of their toes

The currants   strings of pearls
remind him of eggs in ancient oceans
or those jars of embryos in the museum
lit and yellowing
and wired to the branch

While here and there
across this little piece of land
the old men press their heads
against green flanks
and sit bent-backed on their stools
each one alone on his own allotment

A dead man always
has the same appearance—
First the blossom
then the rot

He breathes particulates
cloudy spirits swirl
Call them midges   gnats
dust specks
Call them matter

Bone Monkey applies for a job in forensic acoustics

Her ad in the paper attracts his attention: Actors wanted to simulate death cries for Research Project, Dept. Linguistics. She sets up equipment and plays him a medley of 999 calls where voices are heard through a phone dropped on tarmac or thrust in a pocket. "Listen to this segment here—It's come from deep pain, direct from the heart, I want you to mimic a genuine death cry." She asks him to pick out a voice script, a room for rehearsal. He settles himself by the desk and gets comfortable, opens his briefcase, pulls out his mobile, and plays the last video—the screen a dim flutter of image and shadow: "Who are you? For God's sake don't do this!" Then "Jesus" and "No" repeated, diminished. Vowels like a ligature knotted with consonants.

Now he stands at the microphone and breathes from his diaphragm and slowly, lightly performs a vocal slide then tosses some sounds "pah," "bah," "kah," "gah". She stands in the doorway, with iPhone and clipboard. "Have you chosen a script? Are you ready to start?"

Bone Monkey in Illyria;
an English Gentleman Abroad 1846

1. *An Off-the-shoulder Number*

He reams our ears
till burrs of bone
and curls of wax
lie on his palm—
little light feathers

*

went out riding at three
towards the mountains
on the right/
across the ferry through
beautiful Oak under-woods

*

blow with a soft breath
across his palm
to set those feathers
up
with the dust motes

*

bears and deer
frequent these woods/
tracks near the brook/
a magnificent thunderstorm
came up from the south west

*

blow
with a soft breath
then breathe in
Continue
as if you mean it

*

the woods are chiefly Ash and Oak
and from the summits
and clefts in the rocks/
Italian Pines shoot out in every direction –
the lilac also grows here in profusion

*

through the thunder
a blackbird's
liquid
voice—
You are riding

*

splendid forked lightning
and three or four crashing
claps of thunder/
the echoes continue rolling
round the mountains for several minutes

*

into the blue mountains
through beautiful
Oak under-woods
listening   listening—
a very pretty ride

2. On Speaking with the Natives
—Tower of Skulls at Niš, Serbia—

Mr Gutch and I spent days with the Archbishop
drinking spirits of wine and aniseed and cold water.
We could not refuse the dinners, twenty-six dishes,
the apricots and cherries, the cucumbers—

beaded and chilled and sprinkled with salt.
The fields make bitter black bread here.
The people stare. One night we walked from the Palace
to the Tower of the Skulls and met Stevan Sinđelić.

It's easy to climb the Tower of the Skulls,
we are only visitors, after all, and our bellies are full.
But the flesh of his head had been shipped to the Sultan,
and he clattered like a stork from his bone white tree.

I've stolen the skull of Stevan Sinđelić
though his teachings must come third hand to me—
to the dragoman in Serbian, to Mr Gutch in Italian,
and from he to me in English, so I may understand.

We trot towards Dover under the star-light—
the passion is on him, pitching and tossing,
and tied to my saddle. But all he can tell me,
comes down in the end to blood, a battle, and dying.

3. My Red Morocco Jack Boots

There are seven stations between Belgrade and Alexnitza
where changing horses takes an hour. At Pashapolanca
we had bread and slivovitz then lay on hard board
and slept very soundly. In white caps and German blouses,

Turkish trousers, with twelve yards of stuff, and jack boots
(mine were red morocco) our cavalcade moved off.
At night the path was very striking, summer lightning
pierced the dense foliage. I am not a Romantic

but here and there we came suddenly upon
encampments of caravans from Stambul and glimpsed
the wild forms of shadow men around a blazing fire.
At one such place I left my companions

these travel notes being all I took. They blundered
onwards to their next hotel, a consul dinner
in a dirty town, while I dismounted gesturing
and asking, in English, for the local wine.

These days I while away my time in idle pleasures
for the men are very sociable and well disposed.
I found a good specimen of a Serbian woman,
alone in the woods on her way to market,

her hair dyed black and twisted to one side;
she wore, like the Greeks, a tight under vest,
a purple velvet jacket, embroidered in gold and silver,
a treble row of ducats around her neck

and a silk petticoat which slipped through my fingers
like the river Morava. A practical woman,
she saw what I wanted, and opened her legs
by the side of the mountain, saying nothing.

Vespula Vulgaris

Where are you wandering to, little fools
Come, big sister will teach you how to write verse
Itchy little wasps sucking rotting flowers
Wasps
    —Ho Xuan Huong, translated by Marilyn Chin

The queen of wasps
Sips honey through a straw
Winter comes on
Death hovers by her door

when she wakes
he soft-boils an egg
and parts her lips with a spoon

yolk lines a lip crease
he loosens the edges with his nail
picks at the oily flakes

he puts three spoons of sugar in her tea
clips on the beaker lid
and offers her the straw

Here's a pretty stick
To put upon her lip
Cored of its pith
And parched of its sap

Is this what time does—
smears a memory
across her face?

it's held
then dropped
butterfingers he thinks

and slides the tips of his fingers
into the softness
of her facial hair

the trembling
of her upper lip's a draught
crossing a spiders web

if he could love her
he would love
this clarity

Clarity—
What's that?
Time
To forget

a breeze at the open door
flutters at hem and at the buttoned seam
of the dress he's put on her

and out in the garden under the leaning plum
above the ragwort and the dock
wasps are scouting lacquered gold and black

the spilt grains on the table
draw them in
her glazed lips and her teeth ajar

are half-closed doors they cluster at
with feet like dancers' feet
they find a purchase on her lips

In tenderness she draws
Venom to his tongue
She sucks the last sweet drops
Returns them as a song

He's Hades to her Persephone—
they play a silent game these days
there's not much left

of what she was, she eats, sleeps
defecates and sometime sings
short well-remembered phrases,

hymns to celebrate the autumn rites—
a sudden blaze of light
a cornucopia

of straw-gold fruits
then silence, silence, silence
Does she remember him?

His world's a rookery
He caws. The other rooks reply
Their cruel beaks' susurrus
Chafes her as they sway

sometimes he thinks it's all an act
and she's intact but buffered from the world,
her eyes blank windows to a sumptuous feast

where he's the gardener, his face pressed up
against the glass, to catch her take
the rich meat of a nectarine

He strings her up
With gut or wire or silk
Hung by her neck
She cannot speak

then he's a grinning ape
playing her synapses—
a harpist of unusual virtuosity,

a bone-thin workman with a sly look
and a jack plane, shavings so sheer
they curl like tissue at her feet

a hangman in a tattered vest
with rope and rule and jotter pad
measuring the drop

He's busy in her nest—
So many mouths to feed
He'll prick their jellied
Throats to make them bleed

later he sinks down with her
tongues the salty gathers in her neck
the sour yeasts in greasy hair

he prods her teats
that hang from thin flaps
pasted to her ribs

and sets her limbs
to let them fall aslant
as if in sleep

she stirs, mumbles
an incoherent phrase
and slips away again

He suckles her
As outside in the sun
She mines
The cavities of plums

he sees the exits and the entrances
the open window and the cirrus sky
a halting breath like any other

its drone now loud now falling to a sigh—
a rookery in a copse of autumn light
a distant murmur before the fall of night

On Your Back

bone monkey is on your back
everything sold/ everything old
everything old sold
everything cold

even this path/ even this path
even this path reminds you
trees can be so/ trees can be/ trees can sough
even this path/ even this path
near water/ near cover / near cloud

even here bone monkey is on your back
loud louder loudest listen
bone monkey has hands on your ears
his face against yours
his open mouth his SHOUT
his fingers over your ears

even this path/ even this path
his path/his trees/his clouds/ your back
your back/ your back/ your heavy back
his fingers his clever fingers
even here bone monkey is on your back
even here/ even on this path

The Southern Swallowtail

what he likes is the lie of it
the upside-downness
striped black and white

how it's open
cut through, but reversed—
the husk of a flower

Assemblage des Beautés

Bone monkey has set up shop in the airing cupboard.
It's warm in there. Silverfish take refuge in his skull
and slide around his ribs. Worn sheets have ruched between
his bones like the petals of old roses—*Assemblage des Beautés*
for instance—so cherry red and full it almost seems
there is blood again and a heart beating like crazy.

Post Laborum Gratissima Quies

In Umbria, where the trees talk to each other,
screech scratch, screech scritch,

the stones under his feet, the cicadas,
the dry leaves, ants making their way

who knows where, are silent.
There's no place he'd rather be than here—

blurred as the cockerel's cry,
as a tin bell clanging the quarter hour.

On their knees in the heat
the scabs of hill top farms, olive groves,

fields where a harvest has been gathered,
corn, sunflowers. He's seen the buzzard's

under-wing alight, the feathers traced with gold,
the talons folded, like a woman's, after work.

He adopts the posture of a stool pigeon

Keeping his head bent low he coos
I take the blame for everything
although his eyes are buttonholed

and sewn. Slicked down
with oil his skull shows off
its parting with a smile.

He nestles sweetly in your hand.
Traitor of traitors.
Calling down the hawks.

Fire and fleet and candle-lighte
(Lyke-Wake Dirge)

Not knowing how to die he hits the sack
and curls in foetal pose, pretends he's dead.
His bed's a table tomb tonight. It's dark,
his heels and elbows clatter on the slab.

He'd pray, if prayers were what it took, for signs
that death is imminent. Christ! What he'd give
for silence and an end to everything.
But still his ruthless heart beats on. He lives.

If lardy man can die, then why can't he?
Like alabaster effigies turned to stone,
sappy with youth, or mealy mouthed with age,
a moment's inattention and they're gone.

He lights a candle, lustrous in the dark.
Then with his thumb and finger stubs it out.

The pond in summer

all the trees in the meadow
are swimming dressed in silk

fisher boys line the banks
the water is viridian and lime

both slick and lucid
charcoal daubs

slew
in the sediments

*

oxygen saturates this ward
there is great danger of explosion
and water has penetrated the walls

the ceilings are criss-crossed
with beetle tracks

his wife's mouth is concealed
by her sharpened teeth—
she has accepted silence—

with dentures adrift
he talks and talks

*

all the trees at the margin
are swimming dressed in net

fisher boys line the banks
the water is viridian and sage

mist feathers the surface
beak under wing

drakes
drift at their mooring

*

the grating of sound
through the larynx
and all that granular wearing away

of rock on rock
to scree

when he grinds his teeth
fricatives and sibilants shoot out—
only the outrageous

absences are stones
in his stomach

*

all the trees in the mirror
are swimming dressed in ice

fisher boys line the banks
the water is viridian and slate

pitching small stones
the darkened glass

bobs
and its forest quakes

*

his urine finds its way by dribs and drabs
from slackened penis to transparent bag

a tether at his wrist draws down a flood
of salty liquor *It won't hurt* they said

opening a vein to water down his blood
his anus buds a haemorrhoidal bloom

a wavering O extrudes a thread
through wizened cheeks   a coughed perfume,

a musky hum that marks him as he makes his bed.
He floats   he calls her   but she won't come.

*

all the trees in the meadow
are swimming dressed in fur

fisher boys line the banks
the water is viridian and rose

the pike are lazy
larval midges rise

slewed
in its sediments

Notes:

Bone Monkey applies for a job in forensic acoustics

In BBC Radio 4's 'The Call' (1st March 2011), Professor Peter French of the University of York talked about the art and science of forensic acoustics, including speaker profiling, voice line-ups, and sound enhancement.

Bone Monkey in Illyria; an English Gentleman Abroad 1846

These poems are based on the travelogue diary of George Sydney Davies (1822–1895) Solicitor Registrar of the County Court and Clerk to the Justices Commissioners of Taxes (Davies & Son) Crickhowell, my great, great grandfather who travelled with Mr Gutch to Serbia in 1846. However the events described in this work are fictitious.